THE Power OF Storytelling
IN Worship AND Education

JED GRISWOLD

THE Power OF Storytelling IN Worship AND Education

A PRACTICAL GUIDE

WOOD LAKE

Editor: Mike Schwartzentruber
Proofreader: Dianne Greenslade
Designer: Robert MacDonald

LIBRARY AND ARCHIVES CANADA CATALOGUING IN PUBLICATION
Title: The power of storytelling in worship and education : a practical guide / Jed Griswold.
Names: Griswold, John E., author.
Identifiers: Canadiana (print) 20220174350 | Canadiana (ebook) 20220174369 |
ISBN 9781773435190 (softcover) | ISBN 9781773435206 (HTML)
Subjects: LCSH: Storytelling – Religious aspects – Christianity. | LCSH: Christian
literature – Authorship. | LCSH: Christian education of children. | LCSH: Worship.
Classification: LCC BT83.78 .G75 2022 | DDC 268/.6 – dc23

ISBN 978-1-77343-519-0

Published by Wood Lake Publishing Inc.
485 Beaver Lake Road, Kelowna, BC, Canada V4V 1S5
www.woodlake.com | 250.766.2778

Wood Lake Publishing acknowledges the financial support of the
Government of Canada. Wood Lake Publishing acknowledges the financial support of
the Province of British Columbia through the Book Publishing Tax Credit.

Wood Lake Publishing acknowledges that we operate in the unceded territory of the
Syilx/Okanagan People, and we work to support reconciliation and challenge the legacies
of colonialism. The Syilx/Okanagan territory is a diverse and beautiful landscape of
deserts and lakes, alpine forests and endangered grasslands.
We honour the ancestral stewardship of the Syilx/Okanagan People.

GOLD

Printed in Canada
Printing 10 9 8 7 6 5 4 3 2 1

CONTENTS

AUTHOR'S NOTE

This book has been in development for decades, in part because of life's many tugs and, in part, because, like most important lessons, it has taken time to mature.

Along the way, I had many supporters who encouraged this art of storytelling, including my father, Rev. Dr. Walter H. Griswold, who fostered my curiosity in teaching and learning; and the congregations who listened to my first stories and shared with me their own life stories. These congregations are the Christian Churches (Disciples of Christ) in Hagans and Core, West Virginia; Lake Lynn Chapel in Lake Lynn, Pennsylvania; Central Congregational Church (United Church of Christ) in Newtonville, Massachusetts; and Beneficent Congregational Church (United Church of Christ) in Providence, Rhode Island.

The lessons shared here were first practiced pre-COVID but they are fully applicable to both in-person and virtual environments, since they employ current best practices in education.

Thank you, all.

PROLOGUE

Once upon a time, as a doctoral student in seminary, I was sitting around a conference table for the first session of a Christian education course, wondering how the class would begin. My instructor was Dr. Harjie Likins, an energetic and wise educator, whom I clearly remember all these decades later. She brought a blend of humility and expertise and never bragged about the significant credentials she brought to our class: her dissertation advisor was Reinhold Niebuhr (Dr. Likins would later be *my* dissertation advisor); she was a graduate of Columbia Teachers College; and she had years of accomplished experience in ministry and religious education.

As an opening exercise, she asked us about our approach to the "children's time." I answered, "I use object lessons, of course, since that's what all the Christian education books recommend." She immediately pretended to have stroke! (She had a flair for the dramatic.)

"No! No! No! Just think about it. How have Buddhist monks taught children *and* adults for centuries? And rabbis? And Hindu swamis? And Islamic leaders? And native tribal leaders in lands around the globe? And, oh, by the way ... think about how Jesus taught.

"Storytelling is the way to reach the soul. It's our religious tradition," she concluded.

Her advice echoed wisdom from another teacher of mine, John Westerhoff at Duke University, from my earlier days in seminary, but I was too young, then, to be ready to fully grasp the concept. Now I was *ready* (an important aspect of learning), and Harjie spoke with such heart and conviction, I knew I had to change.

But how? I had used object lessons for nearly two decades, and I was petrified by the thought of challenging an approach everyone else had apparently used and had expected for years. Who was I to do that? And where would I begin?

This book is the one I wish I had back then – a primer on reasons to make that transition and tips for how to do it, based on my personal experience, after more than three decades in ministry since Harjie's class, and over 25 years of college teaching (including courses in educational psychology). It includes 20 samples from the nearly 100 stories I have written to share with children during worship, so you won't have to reinvent the wheel to begin. I have also included a sample lesson plan for teachers.

PART 1

12 Tips for Storytelling

TIP 1

REMEMBER: STORYTELLING IS THE TRADITIONAL GATEWAY TO FAITH

The three Abrahamic faiths share a common foundation in the concept of Torah, which can be translated, at its root, as "story."

Depending on the context in which it is used, it can refer to *part* of the story (such as the Ten Commandments) or to the *whole* story of a people of faith, or according to one teaching from Jesus, it can be summed into one *rule*: "Love thy neighbour as thyself." Whatever its contextual translation, at its heart is a *story*.

Following this tradition, it is appropriate to merge both the goal and the method of story into our religious education in order to

- foster a sense of awe and mystery about the sacred
- address our sacred and secular struggles
- encourage life-long and intergenerational spiritual reflection
- increase self-awareness and other-awareness in our religious traditions

The central, cornerstone stories of our religious traditions have an enduring power because they

- are memorable – and so we ask, in this book, *"What makes a story memorable?"*
- are inclusive – and so we ask, *"What fosters inclusive storytelling and listening?"*
- invite questions (the first step in a life-long process of learning) – and so we ask, *"What story structure best invites questions rather than closes curiosity?"*
- plant seeds for later questions, when listeners are ready to grasp deeper levels of meaning – and so we ask, *"How can a children's lesson foster later questions?"*

The approach to *storytelling* and *story-writing* put forward in this book is based on these goals.

TIP 2

RESPECT THAT CHILDREN GO THROUGH DEVELOPMENTAL STAGES

It was Jean Piaget who first detailed different stages of cognitive development: the "sensorimotor stage" (approximately birth to age two), the "preoperational stage" (approximately ages two to seven), the "concrete operations stage" (approximately ages seven to 11), and finally the "formal operations" stage (ages 12 and above). Of importance for religious educators, Piaget's theory supports the conclusion that object lessons are cognitively appropriate only for listeners at the "formal operations stage," *after* all the other stages have been experienced. Only at the formal operations stage (over age 11) are children usually successful at thinking by analogy. While some psychologists believe that this stage might be breached as early as age eight, most agree that 12 is a more common age at which children are able to cognitively process analogies and metaphors.

In congregations that invite children forward for a children's time, rarely do 12-year-olds join the four-year-olds (which is one reason I recommend *not* inviting children forward; I will address this further in Tip 8).

While object lessons appeal to an older audience, stories appeal to *everyone* in an audience, both cognitively *and* emotionally. But I suspect that if you took a popularity poll comparing object lessons to storytelling, object lessons would win by a landslide. Why? Here's what I think is happening:

- Object lessons are entertaining (even if sometimes at the expense of the children).
- Object lessons can avoid uncomfortable emotions (such as fears), even though they often need to be named and not ignored.
- Object lessons are an "old school" way of teaching by analogy; adults can grasp them and nod affirmingly, even if children aren't ready to understand them.

While some of those things may sound appealing, there are definite downsides:

- Funny reactions can turn into embarrassing moments.
- Emotions are a primary entry point into our favourite movies or novels, and also into our faith. They can be the starting point for the next step – wondering and asking questions.
- Object lessons are often devoid of that emotional invitation.
- Object lessons require cognitive readiness for understanding and thus exclude younger listeners.

While object lessons clearly have a place in education and can be appropriate for older audiences, stories invite listeners of all *ages* and *stages*, and are thus an important addition to the learning process.

TIP 3

ACCOMMODATE DIFFERENT LEARNING STYLES AND PERSONALITIES

No two children are the same and personalities come in different "types" too. Consequently, each child in a group is likely to focus somewhat differently on a given story. Among the key learning styles or personality types relevant here are the "detail-focused learner," the "imagination-focused learner," the "feeling-focused learner," and the "thinking-focused learner."

THE DETAIL-FOCUSED LEARNER
What first captures the attention of the *detail-focused learner* is the way that the details in a story address *what is*, and the way the listener's five senses are engaged through vivid and *practical* detail. Think

about which novels or biographies attract *your* attention and why: perhaps they contain vividly described details (whether significant or incidental) which serve to draw you into the story.

THE IMAGINATION-FOCUSED LEARNER

What first captures the attention of the *imagination-focused learner* are the possibilities inviting the listener's imagination through the sixth sense. Think about which novels or biographies attract *your* attention: perhaps you wonder if *an untold aspect* of a person's life influenced the story; or how the ending *could have been* different, or what *might happen* in a sequel.

THE FEELING-FOCUSED LEARNER

What first captivates the attention of the *feeling-focused learner* is a *subjective* relation to a story and its characters and how they stir a *heart* response, where you feel yourself emotionally identifying and connecting with the characters and what's going on in the story. Think about which novels or biographies attract *your* attention: Is this a character or a story you can identify with? Does that character inspire you, or anger you? What are you feeling, now, as the story unfolds?

THE THINKING-FOCUSED LEARNER

What first engages the attention of the *thinking-focused learner* is an *objective* analysis of the action within the story and its consequences. It is a *head* response that processes concepts and events. Think about which novels or biographies attract *your* attention: What are the consequences of a character's actions? How has the character weighed the advantages and disadvantages of their actions?

OBJECT LESSONS

In object lessons, *relevant* details are limited in number and in quality. Consider a classic object lesson: a toothpaste tube that is squeezed. Children are asked to put the paste back into the tube, which they obviously cannot do. The point of the lesson is then stated: "This is like gossip: once you put the words out, you can't take them back." The moral conclusion is thus clear: "Don't gossip." Additional details – such as pointing out what colour the tube is, describing the texture of the paste, making clear that it is a small or large tube – do not foster questions and can actually shut down the listener and the goal of the story. In other words, details in object lessons rarely inspire significant follow-up questions – such as "what if ...?" – since these are shut down by the conclusion, "so the moral of the story is …"

In addition, object lessons tend to have an unintended negative effect. What will the younger children *remember* about the story? Most likely, it will not be the analogy, but the toothpaste that got all over the floor.

STORYTELLING

Storytelling, on the other hand, can purposefully integrate both detail *and* imagination to great effect. By including lots of detail about a character (taller or shorter, darting eyes, large eyebrows, a sharp sense of smell, nearsighted or farsighted) a story can reach beyond what an object lesson can accomplish. For example, carefully chosen details can

- invite *listener identification* (Wow, that's like *me!*)
- interject humour or curiosity
- help create a setting without shutting down attention, offering information to grab the attention of a detail-interested listener
- foster imagination and wonder ("what if"and "why")
- enable the listener's follow-up questions ("what if that detail changes?")
- encourage the listener to wonder what might happen after the story, and

- empower critical thinking by allowing the listener to distinguish between significant and insignificant details – a lifelong skill

While each listener will have an *initial* response, *all* responses represent essential listening skills, and everyone can expand that initial response, especially when encouraged to "stretch" in all of the described approaches. Compared to object lessons, stories offer more opportunities to engage in all these dimensions, which is why the lesson plan at the end of Part 1 includes facilitating questions about details, imagination, feelings, and thoughts, as a way to process the stories.

TIP 4

USE STORYTELLING TO
ASK QUESTIONS

In Bruno Bettelheim's introduction to *The Uses of Enchantment: The Meaning and Importance of Fairy Tales*, he includes a story about a young child whose mother reads a "Jack and the Beanstalk" story at bedtime. As she tucks the child into bed, the child asks, "Mommy, are there *really* giants?" The mother, wanting to help her child feel safe, is just about to answer reassuringly, "Of course not, Sweetie. You're safe; no giants will bother you tonight," but there is just enough of a pause before she speaks to allow the child to continue, "Because sometimes I *feel* small, like I am surrounded by giants."

Had the mother not waited for the rest of her child's question, or had quickly pronounced a reassuring answer, the conversation that *actually* followed – which began with her invitation "Tell me why and when you feel small ..." – would not have happened. The door to that teachable moment would have been closed, a missed opportunity for a meaningful interaction.

Object lessons are closer to what *could have* happened in that conversation between mother and child – a *closed door* that comes with a defined answer, and often, a concluding moral. On the other hand, *stories* are closer to what *did* happen that night, with an open invitation to follow-up questions, which can be asked in the moment, or later. Why did a certain character do or say that? What happened next? How do I feel? What if? What's next?

In short, *listening* and *asking* are more valuable tools in education than *declaring*. The approach to storytelling and story-writing put forward in this book fosters questions and questioning.

TIP 5

ATTRACT MORE LISTENERS BY USING INCLUSIVE LANGUAGE

Recall the illustration about the child listening to a bedtime story in the previous tip. In Bettelheim's original version, the child was a boy. I paraphrased the story here without mentioning gender because of one Sunday morning years ago, when I told a story whose central figure was a boy – and I had only girls sitting in front of me. I wondered, after the fact, if (or how) they had related to the story. Gender-exclusive language can shut down listening and, consequently, learning.

I realized, then, that I had to do some combination of the following:

🌺 use gender neutral names (Chris, Sal, Pat, etc.)

🌺 use no names at all ("the child")

- use alternating male and female central characters
- use gender-inclusive language throughout the story

The most effective approach to storytelling for children is to use gender-neutral names. This is especially true when the story contains more than one child or central character. If you avoid names and use "the child" when there are multiple characters, you will be faced with the problem of having to find another way to distinguish the characters – such as referring to the "older child" or "younger child" – all of which can become cumbersome and lead to awkward, non-idiomatic uses of language which may be difficult for children to follow.

To be inclusive we also need to pay attention to age, gender identity, social roles, disabilities, and more. Since these differences may be invisible or unknowable to you, consider the possibilities as you create characters and scenarios. Erring on the side of greater inclusion will do no harm, while ignoring the many variations of humanity could push a listener away, even away from God, if stories repeatedly neglect a listener's experience.

TIP 6

CREATE LONG-TERM MEMORIES
FOR LATER LEARNING

Once upon a time, as the pastor of a rural congregation that encouraged (and sometimes simply toler-
ated) my transition to storytelling from object lessons,
we had a "spring cleaning day" with "children" of
all ages (children, parents, and grandparents). I was
working with Shannon, who was eight years old, as
we scrubbed the dust off the walls of the fellowship
hall. Out of the blue (or so it seemed), Shannon asked,
"Was that story about the different-looking squirrel
in the forest a *true* story?"

I actually couldn't remember the story, so I asked
her about it and she recounted, with full detail, the
entire story. I later checked my notes and found that
Shannon was five when she first heard that story. It
was also the *only* time she heard that story.

I learned from that experience that if a story captures the listener's attention, it activates a long-term memory. An active lecture or demonstration in my college classes would also create long-term memories. For years, my nieces and nephews recalled an original story I told to entertain them while babysitting, and if I tried to shorten it in subsequent tellings (it was a long story), they reminded me, in great detail, of what I had left out. Stories foster memories more than object lessons do, and memories are key to learning.

The second thing I learned from Shannon was what happens when *memory* combines with *readiness*. When Shannon was five, the story had its own age-appropriate meaning – it was a silly, attention-grabbing story about forest creatures getting along. It contained enough detail *and* imagination to get it stored into memory for when, at age eight, she was *ready* with a follow-up question in search of a deeper meaning.

What followed that day with Shannon was a fascinating, age-appropriate discussion and exploration of the fundamental religious concept of *myth* ("something that may not have ever actually happened but is *always happening*"). What a fruitful blossom of a seed planted years before!

Shannon benefitted from an early start on understanding "myth" in its best religious sense, with the comprehension that, although the events among the forest creatures never really happened, they are always happening in our human lives, so they are, indeed, stories filled with truth. This realization opened the door to even more questions, and deeper understandings.

The challenge in storytelling for religious education then becomes, "How can I create stories that have multiple levels of truth and meaning – and are memorable for later visits?"

TIP 7

USE STORIES TO HEAL PERSONAL AND CONGREGATIONAL CRISES

It was the developmental psychologist Erik Erikson who coined the phrase "identity crisis" to describe his own experience of finding out that his birth story wasn't actually as he had always been told. That kernel of conflict in his personal life inspired his adaptation of Freud's theory and fostered the first detailed explanation of eight stages of psychosocial development. For Erikson, each stage is guided by a crisis of identity during which we face the challenge(s) of "growing up," that is, growing into a more mature stage of self- and other-awareness. Let's look at the theme of just one of these stages, the autonomy stage: *What do I have control over?*

According to Erikson, this important stage first arises roughly between ages one and three. Think about potty training (often over-emphasized but illustrative here) and having control over our own bodily functions. Think of the sense of maturity and accomplishment when a child masters that task. Erikson knew that this was only the beginning of a lifetime of "what do I have control over" challenges: for example, being in a healthy loving partnership and realizing you can't control your partner's emotions or choices; or trusting others even when you can't control their response; or experiencing a loss of control over some functions and behaviours because of illness or aging.

While the idea of *readiness* helps a storyteller to predict certain age-based crises in an audience (such as the autonomy stage between ages one and three), keep in mind that "Eriksonian crises" can reappear at any age. I remember my 92-year-old mother, who was in a nursing home, having to "let go" rather than "hold on" (Eriksonian terms for this stage) to a degree of independence after three serious falls (and many more stitches) when she tried to walk to the bathroom by herself at night. At that point, she needed to let go of that independence and call a nurse to assist her. Moments of psychosocial growth can happen at any age, as in this example, when we re-visit that first, self-aware experience of struggling with autonomy.

At each of Erikson's eight, life-long stages of growth is a crisis of some dimension that pushes us toward a resolution in the midst of a struggle involving self- and other-awareness. Teaching lessons about such life transitions calls for storytelling. A review of Erikson's stages and of your audience (children and adults) will guide you in choosing themes, and certainly enhance your storytelling.

Importantly, life transitions can be viewed not only in terms of individuals as described above, but also in terms of congregational or community development, such as in the experience of a pastor's leaving or arriving, or in a community crisis such as a fire or flood, or in taking a stand on an ethical issue, and even in dealing with a pandemic – all circumstances in which communities have to come to terms with their own level of control or lack thereof. From this perspective, any event, large or small, that affects an entire congregation can be seen as a congregational struggle with what it has or does not have control over.

As a case in point, I remember the gut-wrenching discovery that a child in my congregation was being abused. This was a child who had listened intently to my stories every week in worship. I had an obligation to address the issue privately and also legally, which meant reporting the abuse to the proper authorities, which I did, but I still felt inadequate seeing the child weekly in the context of church services without somehow safely and confidentially speaking to the questions the child surely had. Was the church a place to be silent in the midst of such pain, to look the other way and pretend these terrible things never happened in our lives? Was the child's worship experience supposed to be silent in the face of a crisis?

In all of this, I faced a crisis myself: what did I have control over, and what could I not control?

It was then that I realized one significant power of storytelling. I knew that I could *not* embarrass anyone or break a confidentiality by directly confronting the issue, but I needed to do *something* pastoral, so I addressed the situation *indirectly* by sharing stories about forest creatures who experienced fear and sought safety. It was in that crisis for *me* that I began to create stories about finding safe places, and safe confidants. I learned that I had some control over the situation – I could discretely offer stories that could be understood on a level deeper than the surface details, and thereby open a door to healing and learning by telling stories about finding safety.

As an added benefit, I was also able to offer the same pastoral care even to the children whose abuse was *unknown* to me, but most likely there and in need of attention.

A WORD OF CAUTION

Storytelling is one of many counselling methods used by licensed therapists. It is critical to know that ministers and educators are rarely also licensed therapists. If faced with something such as abuse, or any range of psychological concerns, it is essential to consult an expert. Storytelling can augment counselling, but never replace it.

TIP 8

MAKE THE "CHILDREN'S TIME" A "FAMILY TIME"

Once upon a time, before I started using storytelling for the children's time in worship, I invited the children to the front and greeted them by asking "How is everyone today?"

The first response I got was, "Well, Mommy and Daddy aren't doing well; they argued in the car all the way to church." On another occasion when I asked, "Who can tell us the meaning of Easter?" a child replied, "It's when the Easter Bunny lays eggs on our front lawn."

W. C. Fields is credited with saying (I'm paraphrasing), "Beware of working with animals or children; you will probably lose." If you try to manage preschoolers, unscripted and unrehearsed when gathered in front of the church, you will lose – and the cost of losing is not *your* face, but the *embar-rassed face* of a child or a parent. I learned that when the two experiences I just shared happened more than once. The "Easter Bunny child" asked me later why everyone laughed *at*, not *with*, the kids; the parents who had argued in the car that morning never sent their child forward again.

For congregations that have a "Safe Place Policy," a fundamental rule is *Thou Shalt Not Embarrass a Child*. It is not safe to put children on display without a rehearsed script or consent to an agreed-upon plan. Object lessons require children to come forward to be close enough to see the demonstration, thus putting them on display. On the other hand, for storytelling, everyone can listen wherever they are. And since storytelling is really an invitation to *all* ages to learn, sharing a story with the children while families are sitting together, with Grandma and Grandpa in the pews, has the following significant advantages:

* It treats children and adults as equals in education and worship. Children often sit with parents during the adult hymns and prayers and responsive readings – and hopefully the sermon; why not have the parents sit with children during the "children's time"?

It creates a shared experience as well as a family-oriented environment for the story, which encourages post-story discussions and the discovery of intergenerational similarities in our spiritual journeys.

TIP 9

INTEGRATE THE "CHILDREN'S STORY" AND THE "ADULT SERMON"

The children's story ought not be a stand-alone, independent part of the overall worship experience. It is often connected to the music, responsive readings, and prayers, but not always to the adult sermon. However, it can be easily integrated into the sermon by using the following *win-win* strategies. The children's story can be used as

* a preface to the adult sermon, suggesting the theme
* the equivalent of the first illustration of the sermon
* an illustration in the middle of the sermon (referencing the story the congregation has already heard)
* a concluding illustration, to wrap up the message

On the matter of including children in the entire worship experience, including the adult sermon, consider the following story.

Once upon a time, a family prepared for its Christmas gathering, a tradition they had observed for many years. They carefully planned all of its significant elements: a moment to remember those who had died since the previous Christmas gathering; a table set elegantly with the best of the family dishes; the traditional "carving" of the turkey; a series of toasts to Christmases past and Christmases future; and, of course, stories from Grandma and Grandpa – all around the table in the main dining room.

But before all of that, and well before the dining table traditions began, the children had been ushered to the basement den, where they had their own "children's Christmas," separate from the family, so they never had a chance to participate in those traditions, which were deemed "adult traditions" and much beyond the understanding of young children. Besides, the children would only be disruptive.

Years passed and the children were now parents themselves, with their own separate family traditions for Christmas. It was difficult to attend all-family Christmas gatherings, since they had their own young children and their own family traditions, which competed for Christmas Eve and Christmas morning. As a result, the all-family tradition faded away.

But when it came time for their first Christmas *without* their own parents, their pastor recommended a reunion of sorts – an all-family gathering on Christmas, celebrating the time-honoured family traditions, with a moment to remember those who had died since the previous Christmas gathering; an elegantly set table; the traditional "carving" of the turkey; a series of toasts to Christmases past and future, and, of course, stories, now from the adults-turned hosts; all around the table in the main dining room.

The children, now adults, looked at each other with puzzled expressions, as if to say, "We never participated in those traditions, so they have no meaning for us. Why should we do that?"

The point of this story? The best way for children to *learn* the traditions of our faith is to be *part of them* – to *participate* in them by observing and partaking in the experience, beginning at an early age. Children absorb traditions by a sort of "psychological osmosis."

Although children will not fully understand the sophisticated meanings of our faith traditions, they will *grow* into an understanding by experiencing them over time. Furthermore, children who participate in worship as they grow into it are more likely to stay connected to the church during their young-adult years.

Research indicates that the following scenario tends to play out in churches where children are sent off to Sunday school instead of remaining in worship, perhaps to avoid having "restless" and "noisy" children present during the "important" elements of worship. Children who are absent for the offering, doxology, anthem, most of the hymns, the pastoral prayers, the announcements of congregational concerns and requests for support of important causes, communion, the sermon, and the benediction, fail to absorb these important traditions. Then at age 12 or 14, right after confirmation, they are told, "You are now an adult member of the church and it's time for you to rejoin the congregation for its meaningful traditions." But these young people, having not been exposed to the traditions as children, find no meaning in the Sunday morning rituals. It's difficult to find roots in the unfamiliar, so they slowly, and sometimes not so slowly, fade away from church. They *might* return when they have children of their *own* and want them to grow up in a Christian tradition, but, alas, the cycle continues and that goal of learning the faith tradition is repeatedly missed.

This cycle can be broken by programming and planning for the presence of children in worship. Storytelling is one significant way to accomplish that, in addition to scheduling Sunday school classes, for all ages, before full congregational worship.

To state the obvious, early childhood experiences influence later adult behaviours. Children whose early lives are more integrated into the traditions of the faith (learned by first-hand experience and participation) will more likely integrate *their* religious education experience with their *family's* religious traditions.

If children stay in worship and participate cognitively and behaviourally, they will feel more invited, respected, and integrated when the *children's story*, directed to them, becomes part of the *adult sermon* as well. A reference to the story will also catch their attention during the "adult" time and reduce the restlessness that adults so often worry and complain about.

In addition, having children help with the offering, light candles with adult help, present plays, etc., can increase the size of the "welcome mat" to our important traditions and break the cycle described above.

TIP 10

USE YOUR OWN FAITH TRADITION TO FIND SAMPLES FOR STORYTELLING

During my Christian education course with Dr. Likins, I asked for advice about where to begin, and she reminded me that I didn't have to reinvent the wheel. The list below is a blend of her suggestions and my own. Although it is not an endorsement of all the expressed beliefs and values of these religious traditions, these are good, accessible resources you can use as style references and starting points:

- Rabbinic tales from Judaism (see https://tinyurl.com/4ju6uapf)
- The parables of Jesus
- Zen stories (see *108 Zen Parables and Stories*, by Olga Gutsol)

- Stories by Rumi, the most widely read poet in the world; an Internet search will reveal his many children's fables
- The parables by Kahlil Gibran
  (see *The Prophet*, and *The Collected Works*)
- Stories from diverse cultures
  (see https://tinyurl.com/3pbtsvvt)

My own journey started at what I call "Storyteller Stage 1," using stories from other sources (such as the ones listed above), being conscious of the need to give credit when I borrowed from a source not in the public domain. Over time, I began my "Storyteller Stage 2" phase, which was to adapt public domain stories. Eventually, I found my own voice, "Storyteller Stage 3," and began to compose original stories that more directly connected my faith perspective, audiences, and our shared contexts. You will find 20 of these original stories in Part 2 of this book.

Becoming a storyteller is a process, and there is no reason to be embarrassed at any stage of learning.

TIP 11

WRITE AND TELL YOUR OWN ORIGINAL STORIES

Here are some additional tips that may help you write and tell your own stories.

- Stories in which children are central characters are always inviting, since the audience can identify with the characters – everyone has (or had) a childhood. Consider common childhood experiences with which everyone can identify.

- Stories about characters from nature are always appealing (forest creatures, clouds, leaves, trees, raindrops, stones, etc.). These are primordial and have captured listener attention for centuries. This is evident from the fables of many cultures.

- Choose ordinary, everyday things and experiences for characters in your stories. The Hassidic Jews believe that everything created by God is sacred;

creating a sense of awe about the world around us is a key contribution of all faiths. Encouraging a wider and deeper perspective about our ecosystems (human and non-human) is a valued religious goal.

- Note that in the set of sample stories in the second part of this book there is some repetition of themes. This happens, in part, because of the repetition of themes in our daily lives (love, respect, understanding, learning, encountering differences, patience, etc.). In addition, the basic messages of our faith *need* to be repeated. "Love thy neighbour" should be repeated often, and when such a lesson appears in different contexts and from different perspectives, children of all ages will learn to appreciate the diversity within and around each simple but deep lesson.

- Develop a "signal phrase" that indicates the story is beginning. For those of a certain age who remember Garrison Keillor's *Prairie Home Companion*, the phrase "It's been a quiet week in Lake Wobegon," shifted the brain and body into "story listening mode." I almost always begin with the simple and traditional, "Once upon a time ..." followed by a brief pause. This allows the neurological and psychological shift into story-time mode.

- Describe the situation and scene (paint a word picture, remembering to use detail) that includes a problem or a potential learning event.

- Create a crisis or encounter within the situation (recall Erikson's belief that a crisis is a "teachable moment").

- Offer a suggestion or an open door for a resolution (such as a possible compromise), but *never* end with "the moral of the story is ... " Allow for open problem-solving using our own faith tradition.

- Memorize at least the outline and central details of your story. If you can't do this, you could bring in a large, unique homemade "Book of Stories" and you could read the story, much like reading a bedtime story.

TIP 12

USE "BEST PRACTICES" IN TEACHING STORY-BASED LESSONS

Here is a list of some suggested "best practices" for storytelling and teaching. Remember that the goal is to invite the listener into a sense of awe or mystery, a sense of self- and other-awareness, and a sense of problem-solving using your faith tradition as a guide.

When processing a story or teaching a class after a story, it is appropriate to encourage and positively reinforce a child's *accurate* observations and *reasonable* conclusions. You can do this in the following ways:

🌱 Ask open-ended questions. ("Tell me more?" "How does that make you feel?" "What was that like?")

- Avoid closed questions, which only require a "yes" or a "no" response. ("Did you like the story?" "Do you feel better now?") Ask, instead, "What did you like most about the story (or character)?" or "What are your feelings about this story?"

- Avoid offering your own conclusions. ("The meaning of the story is ...") Leave the story open for individual interpretation, and allow for questions.

- While *guiding* a listener toward an insight, be careful not to *direct* them. Allow room for the Holy Spirit to nudge a new insight: remember the saying, "Out of the mouths of babes ..."

- Be patient as you listen. While extroverts enjoy rapid back-and-forth talk, introverts prefer time to process questions, so allow for quiet filtering time as you ask questions. When extroverts are dominating the discussion (which can easily happen) ask everyone to think for a few seconds before sharing; this will increase the participation of introverts.

Research on critical thinking in education suggests that there are important questions to ask when examining *any* topic.

- What obstacles are being faced in the story?

- What do we know about the characters/situation? (You can say, "Tell me about the story.")
- What are the effects of a character's actions?
- What different viewpoints are presented in the story? (You can help children explore this question by inviting them to act out different roles in the story, as described below.)
- What is the intended purpose of the story? (Keep in mind that a story may have several legitimate purposes.)

The sample lesson plan provided at the end of Part 1 contains some features that may seem repetitive. This repetition is of educational value for several reasons.

- Structure and consistency foster a fertile environment for learning when they also allow for imagination. The lesson plan is organized with that in mind.
- While adaptability and flexibility have much merit, following a predictable approach each time a story is processed serves two valuable purposes (especially for younger children):
  - It develops a discipline of reflection
  - It nurtures a comfort level with the process since children come to know what to expect

Each lesson plan includes a recommendation to act out the story several times. In my years of doing this, the "acting out" part of the class has been the favourite and perhaps the most fruitful for several reasons.

- Much research from neurological psychology has shown the importance of integrating brain or thought processes with behaviour in the learning process; physical movement fosters learning. And children will love the extra physical fun.

- Acting out a story helps a child comprehend the story's content and it also helps the teacher assess what was heard and what was not heard. Sometimes knowing what a child missed is as helpful as knowing what a child remembered.

- Creating a play with different parts allows the children to see a story from different perspectives. (Be sure to include inanimate objects, such as clouds or storms, as characters; you'll be surprised how well this can serve the lesson.) Opportunities to see different points of view (a key element of learning) increase when children are able to act out a story several times, switching parts.

While these goals present challenges in an age of virtual teaching/learning, they can be achieved. You can consult the teachers in your congregation on best practices with both in-person and virtual teaching.

Also included in the suggested lesson plan are opportunities for collaborative activities, a trend also supported by educational research. Collaborative activities can happen virtually as well as in face-to-face groups. Don't be afraid to include activities of your own design. Reasoned and creative flexibility is part of your own story.

In this regard, consider using craft supplies and other resources than can serve a wide age-range of purposes and users. Also, when drawings are suggested, understand that an adult viewer may not recognize a child's particular drawing of a person or object; ask the child for a description from their point of view. (A wise course of action regardless of the age of the artist!)

The suggested lesson plan outline follows a recommended and reasoned sequence, but time, group size, and teacher experience may require choices regarding the most significant and relevant activities. Know your audience. Their ages and interests, their cognitive levels, their creativity and curiosity are all factors that play a role in effective teaching and desirable outcomes.

Finally, please note that the suggested themes at the top of each of the sample stories in Part 2, include an "other" category. One of the best things about a good story is that it can mean different things to different people at different times and places! Add a category when appropriate.

SAMPLE LESSON PLAN

This is a sample outline of a lesson plan that can be used for each story. It establishes a routine that creates a helpful environment for learning (as described in Tip 12) and is intended as a starting point. Those who have purchased the book may duplicate this lesson plan (see page 59) as needed for use in their own congregation or with their own group.

THINKING TIME

(a time for teachers to listen and for children to critically reflect internally or out loud)

All of these questions can be shared individually, or in pairs or triads first, then shared with the whole group. Working in pairs increases collaboration skills. Read (or repeat) the story, to refresh memories.

1. Encourage listening skills. Ask these questions as they apply to the specific story.
   - "Tell me about the story." (Ask the children to re-tell the story.)
   - List key words on newsprint as the children share the story, for use later as the story is processed.

2. Encourage problem-solving skills.
   - "What problems did the main characters face in the story?"
   - "Have you ever experienced something like this? Can you tell us about it?"
   - If a character in the story goes through changes: "Describe the changes."
   - *Clarify the difference between facts and opinions.* When it comes to debating *facts* (such as how tall are you), the fact with more evidence is correct; when it comes to *opinions* (such as, which colour is prettier), there may be different points of view and different answers. Is this a case of debating fact or opinion? Why? Describe another example of different opinions.
   - Can you share an example of when you chose something in your life? Describe what it felt like.
   - Can you share an example of when a choice was made *for you*? Describe what it felt like.

3. Encourage self-awareness and other-awareness (being aware of thoughts and feelings).
   - Describe how you felt as you heard the story.
   - Describe how each character might have felt.
   - What did you like (or dislike) about the story? Why?
   - How do you feel after hearing the story?
   - Describe what you thought about as you heard the story.
   - What do you think each character in the story was thinking?
   - What were you thinking about when you listened to the story?

4. If a character in the story goes through changes …
   - "Describe what changed in the story from the beginning to the end."
   - "Describe how the character might have felt during the changes."
   - "What feelings changed?"
   - "What feelings stayed the same?"

5. Encourage analytical skills (being aware of consequences).
   - Identify an action and ask, "What was the effect of the character's actions?"
   - What do you think is the purpose of the story?
   - What questions do you have about the story?

6. Encourage imagination.
   * What do you think could happen next if the story had continued?

ACTION TIME

(to encourage varied perspectives, teamwork, memory, creativity, movement)

7. Create a play; act out the story. Do this several times to allow children to play different roles, to gain different perspectives. You will be amazed at how fruitful (and fun) this activity can be.

SHARING TIME

(to encourage communication, collaboration, and appreciation of varied perspectives)

8. Did you think of any new questions after playing different parts from different points of view?
9. Did you discover any new feelings after playing different parts from different points of view?

ACTION TIME

(to encourage creativity, individually or in teams)

These activities can be done as a whole group, or in pairs or small groups. They could all work on drawings at the same time, progressing through the suggested list; or each group could be given a different assignment.

10. Draw a picture about the story.
11. Write a poem about the story. (If the group hasn't learned to write yet, they could speak the lines as the teacher writes them on newsprint.)
12. Create a craft project about the story.

SHARING TIME

(to build a sense of group identity and a point of entry for newcomers)

13. Invite children to share the pictures, poems, or projects with a friend in the class by telling a story about it (take turns). Ask children to explain their creative work and how it retells the story.
14. Take a series of pictures (individual and group poses) of the children and their projects. Add

this to an ongoing wall of pictures, or to a scrapbook of pictures, which in the future can be the source of stories to share for reflection, or as a way of welcoming a new class member.

15. Conclude with, "What will you remember about this story?"

PRAYER TIME

(to secure the day's learning in our religious roots)

16. "Thank you, God, for this special story and for the special stories we each bring to the group, and for what we learn when we share."

17. Invite children to add their own comment to the prayer.

18. Conclude with, "Thank you, God, for listening to our own stories as we listen to your stories about Jesus, Creation, and about caring for all the living beings in your beautiful world."

🌿 🌿 🌿

To download a printable version of this Lesson Plan in PDF or Word format, go to: http://www.woodlake.com/storytelling

PART 2

Sample
Stories

THE CAT WHO GREW OLD

THEMES
- Aging
- Loss
- Disabilities
- Communicating without words
- Other:

Once upon a time, there lived a kitty cat and a human who loved each other very much.

Pat, the human, made sure that Kat, the kitty, had enough food and water, a clean litter box, and a safe place to play and explore. And Kat made sure to share cuddles and nudges and sparkling-eyed looks. Each was expressing a special love for the other, and that made everyday life very special.

Time went by and Pat and Kat grew older and changed, but one thing was constant – a special way that they expressed their love, in addition to their caring actions. Pat would look into Kat's eyes and, with a wink, say slowly and in a soft tone, "I love you." And Kat would purr.

But then, things changed even more.

Kat became deaf and could not hear the words, "I love you."

"Is there a way to say 'I love you' without words?" Pat wondered – and then decided to continue to mouth the words. Whenever Kat voiced a lonely meow, wishing to somehow break the silence, Pat would lie down next to Kat to get as close as possible to look into Kat's eyes and, with a gentle touch, say the words "I love you," just like always. Even if Kat could not hear the words with kitty *ears*, perhaps Kat could hear with a kitty heart.

And Kat would look back and begin to purr.

Pat thought, "I wonder if God sometimes breaks the silence by saying 'I love you' without using words?"

CLIMBY THE CATERPILLAR

THEMES
* Overcoming fears
* Overcoming limitations
* Easter
* Other:

Once upon a time, though not that long ago, there lived a caterpillar named Climby. Climby loved to eat green leaves but there was a particular green leaf that Climby *really* enjoyed. It was very tasty, with lots of fibre, so it made an ideal, healthy, midday snack. Climby dreamed every night about finding another tree with these special leaves.

But there was a problem.

These very special leaves only grew at the very, very top of very, very tall trees. And Climby was afraid of heights. Every now and then, with lots of help from friends, Climby would pick a tree and climb very slowly, then, before reaching the top, crawl back down to the ground. After a while, with the help of friends, Climby would try again, climbing a little higher. Finally, Climby reached the top of the tree.

The view was breathtaking, in more ways than one. The beauty and the height took Climby's breath away. Climby's friends offered encouraging and reassuring support. "Take slow deep breaths, and don't look down," they suggested.

The leaves at the top of the tree were indeed awesome and worth the frightening climb. But after enjoying the meal, Climby wondered on the way down, "Will I *ever* get over this fear?"

About that time, Climby looked up just in time to see a bird and a butterfly flying gracefully near the top of one of those special trees.

And Climby wondered ...

THE CLUBHOUSE

THEMES
- 🌿 Neighbourhood clubs
- 🌿 Prejudice
- 🌿 Courage
- 🌿 Excluding and including
- 🌿 In-groups and out-groups
- 🌿 Other:

Once upon a time, though not too long ago, and, in fact, not too far from here, there was a neighbourhood where it seemed like everyone had a special friend, and where every yard was shared for summer or after-school games. On any given day, someone's yard became a ballpark, or the north pole, or an imaginary castle, or an unexplored forest. It was indeed a special neighbourhood.

One day, someone's yard became a prehistoric island, and the children were deciding which parts they would play. It was so much fun that one of the children used the word "club" to refer to the neighbourhood, even though it wasn't *officially* a club.

One of the kids, Robin, said out loud, "Why don't we make it official? With members and even a clubhouse?"

The idea caught on. With help from some adults, plans were drawn up for a clubhouse. Adults would help build and paint it. The children invented secret passwords and secret handshakes. The thought of being able to meet inside a clubhouse with just their friends seemed very special, indeed.

About that time, a new kid, named Dakota, moved into the neighbourhood. Being new, Dakota didn't know the secret passwords and handshakes, and the other children kept Dakota at a distance. Some of them even started calling Dakota names – behind Dakota's back at first, but later, face to face. None of the names were nice.

This bothered Robin, who had the idea of making the clubhouse in the first place. Robin knew that calling Dakota names wasn't right but didn't know what to do about it.

Until one day, it happened.

It was a bright sunny day, a day like today,★ and Robin was with the club members walking down the street toward a yard where they would play. Today, the yard was going to be a new planet just recently discovered. They were walking down the street and Dakota was walking on the *other* side of the street. Robin sensed that somebody was about to start name-calling. Right then something inside tugged at Robin's head and heart, and Robin knew what to do. Darting across the street, Robin approached Dakota and started asking about school, and hobbies, and previous homes before moving here, and other questions to get to know Dakota.

After a few minutes – Robin and Dakota didn't even notice it at first – the rest of the children had moved across the street and had joined them. Off they all went to explore the new planet – and to talk more about expanding the club to include new neighbours.

When appropriate (and possible), connect details from your story to your immediate environment. Describing the weather as a "day like today" makes the story more relatable.

THE DROP OF WATER

THEMES
- ❧ The ecosystem
- ❧ Environmental connections
- ❧ Making our own contributions to the larger world
- ❧ Life changes
- ❧ Other:

Once upon a time, there was a small drop of water who lived in a *very* large ocean. The drop of water *loved* being a part of such a large and diverse community. It could swim with little fish and giant whales; it could share in the fun of big waves and tiny bubbles; and it could find some peaceful rest by diving deep or even by sunbathing near a quiet spot on top of the ocean.

That's just the way it was – until *everything* changed.

The little drop of water found itself being drawn toward a cloud. It didn't understand how or why it had changed, and it thought to itself, "This is it – my life is over!"

But the little drop found that being part of a cloud was pretty cool – the view was breathtakingly beautiful, and the ride was amazingly comfortable.

And then ...

The drop of water which had become part of a cloud changed *again* and became a droplet of water once more. And it began to fall. At first, it thought it was returning to the ocean, until it realized that it was raining upon a field of vegetables (though it wasn't really sure what a vegetable even was). Once again, it thought to itself, "This is it – my life is over!"

While landing on the ground wasn't as bumpy as the drop expected, it didn't understand why it had landed on ground instead of in the ocean. But as it visited with the vegetable plants, the drop of water quickly learned how important it was for the plants and for the nearby creatures (including humans).

As the sun smiled down upon the little drop of water, it sensed that there were more changes to come, but this time the drop of water had a wide-eyed view of how many changes can happen in a life.

FIND-AND-SEEK

THEMES
- ❧ For a leaf-covered, fall day
- ❧ Getting found
- ❧ Being lost
- ❧ Halloween
- ❧ Other:

Once upon a time, a very, very long time ago – about the middle of last week – a group of children celebrated the arrival of a fall by playing hide-and-seek. The air was crisp and cool, the perfect kind of weather for an adventure. Nearby there was a yard with a perfect place to hide: a huge pile of colourful, dry leaves.

Hiding there would also be good practice for Halloween, since you could suddenly pop out of the leaves to give someone a good scare.

God noticed that the children were having so much fun that an announcement was posted on heaven's calendar: "Ghosts and angels will play hide-and-seek this Saturday."

But there was a problem.

Angels and ghosts are hard to see. When they played hide-and-seek, none of them got found.

And so it was that some new rules were made for playing hide-and-seek in heaven. They no longer play "hide-and-seek," they play "find-and-get found" because each one of God's critters, including all of us, deserves to be found.

THE FOREST FIRE

THEMES
- Teamwork
- Safety through cooperation
- Other:

Once upon a time, there was a forest filled with all kinds of creatures, including birds that could fly as high as the sky, woodchucks that could dig deeper than tree roots, and moose with antlers so strong they could knock down trees.

On most days the forest was a pleasant and safe place for the creatures to live. The birds, woodchucks, and moose all had their own space, and they respected the space of the others.

But one day that all changed.

No one knew how or why the fire started, but it quickly became a ferocious and dangerous threat to everything that lived in the forest.

None of the creatures knew what to do – at least, not at first. To make matters worse, they rarely spoke to each other, since they stayed in their different spaces and spoke different languages.

Then it happened.

The wise old owl, who was trusted by all, signalled, with a wing-wave and an owl-stare, an emergency meeting, and everyone volunteered to help.

The birds would fly high above the fire to alert the others to its path, and to find a safe way out of the danger zone. The woodchucks would dig the deepest tunnels they could to provide a safe place to hide from the fire until it was over, for those who *couldn't* find a way out. And the moose would use their antlers to knock down big trees to build a temporary barrier for the flames.

And most of the forest animals survived to tell the story. After that, the forest became an even *more* pleasant and safe place to live.

THE FOUR WEATHERS

THEMES
- Taking your turn
- Patience
- Respect for others
- Differences
- Other:

Once upon a time ... a very, very long time ago, there lived four weathers.

Winter was blustery and enjoyed surprises. It was filled with enthusiasm and always ready to jump into the scene, day or night, with such energy that it almost blew over the other weathers with its cold gusts of wind.

Summer was just about the opposite. It was soft-spoken and sometimes a little lazy, trying to linger on the scene in a quiet way. And, unlike winter, summer enjoyed longer days and more variety like rain and clouds, and hot sun and cool winds.

Spring was different because it liked to be predictable and organized, so that seeds could develop through their stages of growth, to blossom into bright pinks and yellows and blues.

And then there was fall, who also liked pretty colours but preferred darker shades of browns and reds and oranges. It also enjoyed cooler temperatures. And fall liked leaves to drop to the ground rather than reach to the treetops.

But there was a problem.

The four weathers were not good at taking turns, because this happened so long ago that taking turns had not been invented yet.

So God called a meeting of the four weathers and taught them about taking turns.

And the four weathers became the *four seasons*.

FROGGY AND THE NEW YEAR

THEMES
- The first day of school
- Advent
- New Year's Day
- Making every day a special day
- Other:

Once upon a time, there lived a frog named Froggy.

Froggy was an ordinary name, but Froggy was no ordinary frog. However, Froggy *did* live in a rather ordinary *pond*.

One day, about this time of year, on a day that was very much like today, a rather interesting discussion took place around the pond. One group of lily pads said quite clearly that there was something different in the air.

"It *smells* different. It even *feels* different. It must be the beginning of a new year," they all called out together.

Some of the dragonflies (who liked to visit the pond because of its edible and tasty flies) replied, "Oh, no, no, no. It's the first day of spring; you can tell because of all the new flies near the pond – new flies are what mark the beginning of a new year. When spring begins, so does a new year."

Then some fish who happened to be swimming nearby said, "Oh, no, no, no. It's the beginning of school that marks the start of a new year." (Perhaps that's why a group of fish is called "a *school* of fish.")

Just then a "*Sunday* school of fish" swam by. They remembered their Sunday lessons and said, "Oh, no, no, no. It's not the first day of Spring, and not when school begins, it's *Advent* that marks the beginning of a new year."

After quietly listening, another dragonfly spoke up, saying, "Oh, no, no, no. It's a birthday that marks the start of a new year." (Perhaps it was that dragonfly's birthday.)

At that point, Froggy thought out loud, "Hmmm. Since every day is a *new* day, perhaps *every* new day is the beginning of a new year. I think I shall make this New Year's Day today very special."

GRANDMA'S STORIES

THEMES
- Death of a grandparent
- Loss
- Family changes
  (divorce, moving, etc.)
- Other:

Her face was very wrinkled – perhaps because of age, perhaps because a face can often add a wrinkle for every wise wondering.

Her grandchildren loved her very much, but they never quite understood the cause of her wrinkles. Wrinkled sheets, yes. Wrinkled paper, yes. But her wrinkled face? It was still a mystery.

Her age was another mystery. The numbers were pretty big. Some of her grandchildren couldn't even count that high yet, and well … it was just hard to imagine how old 50 might be, or 60, or 70, or even 80 or 90!

So her age and her wrinkles – they were both a mystery.

But there was one thing that was *not* a mystery. The children knew that every holiday Grandma would share stories of "the old days." Most of the time, the grandchildren didn't really listen very closely, because they had heard the stories before and they knew they would hear them again.

But this holiday* was different.

It was the first holiday* without *Grandpa* and when Grandma began to tell her old stories again, they seemed … well … different. And new.

Perhaps it was that Grandma had changed; perhaps because there was a new wrinkle on her face. Or perhaps it was because the children listened differently.

Whatever the reason, the children *did* listen very closely. They even asked some questions. Then they even shared some stories of their own, just like Grandma.

And so although it was different it was also the same. And the time they all spent together was still special.

*or family gathering

LEE THE LEAF

THEMES
- 🍁 Matthew 20:1–16
- 🍁 Equality in heaven
- 🍁 Equality on earth
- 🍁 Fall
- 🍁 Other:

Once upon a time a very, very long time ago, about this time of the year, God decided to have a big party. So, naturally, God needed to decorate the heavens.

It was the time of year when the air was turning cooler, and the sunlight was somehow softer. God looked all around for interesting colours that could be gathered for the decorations and noticed the leaves, which were beginning to display just about every colour the angels could imagine. So God sent a strong wind to knock down some of those leaves, and then God called to them: "I want you to come to my party."

Then the wind blew again, making more leaves fall into what was now a *huge* pile.

But there was a problem.

Lee the leaf didn't want to go to a party. Lee wanted to keep hanging on tightly to a branch. Perhaps Lee was afraid of falling or didn't know what to expect at the party. Or maybe Lee just enjoyed the company of a frequent visitor, a local caterpillar.

Another wind blew by and Lee heard the voice again: "I want you to come to my party." More leaves began to fall.

Finally, Lee was the only leaf left on the tree. A last gust of wind was all it took. Lee let go and landed right on top of the huge pile of leaves at the base of the tree.

Then God began to collect the leaves for the party, and all the leaves finally knew the plan.

As the last leaf to fall, Lee was the first leaf God picked up. Some of the leaves who came to the pile of "party leaves" first began to mumble, "We responded to the invitation *first*, so we should be *picked up* first."

But when they got to God's party, they all forgot who was first and who was last.

LONNY THE LEAF

THEMES
- 🌿 Changing seasons at fall
- 🌿 Changes in life
- 🌿 Sharing
- 🌿 Letting go
- 🌿 Dealing with loss, death
- 🌿 Other:

There was once a young child named Taylor. Taylor's favourite expression was, "It's mine, it's mine. I won't let go." Taylor always said this with hands clenched, and eyes and ears closed to anyone who would say anything else.

One day, an older and wiser child named Robin said, "You know, it really is okay to let go sometimes. It might even be a relief."

Taylor said, "I don't understand. Tell me more."

So Robin told a story ...

Once upon a time there was a leaf named Lonny.

Lonny was a regular leaf who liked regular leaf things: swinging in the breeze, waving at birds and butterflies, watching raindrops, and listening to humans who stopped by to rest at Lonny's tree trunk. (Most humans don't know this, but leaves have hidden ways to sense everything that happens around them.)

But there was a problem.

Lonny didn't listen well. So when the wind started whispering, "It's fall, Lonny ... so *fall, Lonny*," Lonny missed the message.

And when the weather started to change and the days started to grow shorter and the wind's voice got louder and other leaves started to let go, Lonny, eyes and ears closed, held on tight.

"I *won't* let go. I'll *never* let go."

Lonny got stiffer and stiffer in the cold weather, but still held on. Even when a piece of cover for the tree, named Bark, barked out to Lonny, "Let go, Lonny ... let go," Lonny held tight.

And then it happened.

Lonny finally let go. The trip down was an unexpected adventure. No longer stiff and tight, Lonny flew gently like a bird, and slowly like a butterfly, to join a great party of children playing in the pile of leaves at the base of the tree.

Taylor listened intently to Robin's story and wondered ...

LOOK UP, LOOK DOWN, LOOK STRAIGHT AHEAD

THEMES
- Luke 24:13–27
- Paying attention to our surroundings
- Other:

Once upon a time, a very long time ago, in a town very near Jerusalem, there lived two very curious children.

One of them was named Cleopas, but we don't know the name of the other. They were both very curious about the problems of growing up, like "Why do bad things happen to good people?" and "What am I going do when I am older?"

They wondered about these things and spoke together about them often. One day, they decided to ask three wise teachers in their village, hoping to find some answers.

The first teacher said, "Whenever you have questions that trouble you, you must raise your eyes toward the heavens, and there you will find your answers."

The second teacher said, "Whenever you are worried, you must keep your eyes low to the ground, toward your feet, so you won't stumble."

The third teacher paused for a moment and then said, "The first two teachers are correct. You should look up *and* you should look down. But in-between, you must look straight ahead, as well."

Many years passed. The two children, now adults, were still close friends, and now they were followers of Jesus.

Then, one day, something bad happened. Jesus died. They had heard some talk about "resurrection," and they were confused about what that meant.

Once again, they had lots of questions, just like when they were children. They decided to go for a walk to talk about it because sometimes walking while talking helps.

While they walked, Cleopas prayed and looked to the heavens, like the first wise teacher had suggested. Cleopas' friend, whose name we don't know, followed the advice of the second wise teacher and just looked at the ground while walking.

They both forgot the advice of the third wise teacher to look straight ahead.

That's when it happened.

A stranger appeared. Had they been looking straight ahead they would have known who it was, but they had only been looking up or down. As soon as they looked straight ahead, they saw that the stranger was Jesus.

"Look straight ahead, and let me tell you about what has happened," Jesus said.

THE POWER OF A SAFE PLACE

THEMES
- Being safe
- Safe places
- Feeling in control
- Other:

Once upon a time, not very long ago, in fact very recently *and* close to home, there was a very still evening.

So still that the birds forgot to sing.

So still that even the leaves hung motionless, like in a photograph.

It was very quiet and peaceful.

Until the storm came.

And what a storm! It announced itself with such sudden fury that the birds, the forest animals, and the humans all scattered for safety. Several children were still playing in the yard and their first instinct was to run into the kitchen, where they spent so much time and felt safe. But there were lots of windows in the kitchen, and every flash of lightning, and every boom of thunder, and every gust of strong wind rattled the window frames, which frightened them even more.

They didn't feel very safe, and at that moment feeling safe was important.

Then, they had an idea.

They must have all thought of it at the same time, because together they all moved toward the *safe place*. They had gone there before, sometimes alone, sometimes together. It was a place where they kept special things – a beautiful rock, a card from a grandparent, a stuffed animal, a really old toy that was just too special to throw away ...

It was just the perfect place to be during a scary storm.

In that place, they felt safe. They also felt a strange but comforting sense of power. Not power over the storm, but power over their fear. They felt like they were in control of themselves *inside*, even when the storm *outside* seemed to be out-of-control.

They stayed in their safe place while the storm raged, knowing that eventually it would go away, but the power of their safe place would remain.

THE PRETTIEST COLOUR OF ALL

THEMES
- Diversity
- Appreciating different points of view
- Other:

One day, a very young child asked a very old but very wise adult, "Why are there so many colours in autumn?" The older adult thought for a moment (a sign of wisdom at work), and then told this story.

Once upon a time, God decided to hold a contest to choose the prettiest colour of all. Because this was a big job, God delegated an angel to oversee the contest. Very quickly, word spread that all the colours that had ever been created were to gather together, all in neat rows, so that the angel could pick the most beautiful colour of all.

And so every colour – the forest greens of summer, and the softest lawn greens of fall; the brightest yellows of the canaries, and the brownish yellows of the fall leaves; the bright reds of poppies and the pink reds of sunsets; the deep, dark greys of storm clouds and shadowy greys of dusk; the deep blues of the ocean and light blues of a sunny summer sky – every colour that had ever been seen showed up at the appointed time. Then they all lined up so that there was a neat row of reds, and there was a neat row of blues, and a neat row of yellows, and ... well, there were enough lines of colour so that every colour had a place.

The angel looked at all the colours but couldn't decide which was prettiest because they were *all* so pretty.

Finally the angel sighed and said, "I can't decide ... I need to take a break while I think it over."

Since the angel was taking a rest, the colours decided they would take a rest from standing in lines too, and they started mingling and mixing.

That's when the angel had an idea. The angel thought, "Since all the colours are so beautiful, I think God should shuffle them all together."

So that's what God did. God created autumn, when so many beautiful colours become even *more* beautiful when they are mixed, separate yet together – the brights and the softs, the bold and the gentle – side by side, together long enough to enjoy before the first winter storm.

REACHING OUT

THEMES
- Friends and neighbours
- Support
- Growing
- Other:

Once upon a time, not so long ago and not very far away, there lived a cucumber seed named Q.

In spite of being very small, Q had very big dreams of being the largest, tastiest cucumber ever. So Q drank in as much water and sun as it could, and even did stretching exercises to grow stronger. Exactly what kind of stretching exercises those were is still a mystery, but for sure Q was doing everything it could to live up to its dream.

Everything was going well, including being very hopeful, until ...

One day, Q noticed how heavy a fully grown cucumber could be, watching how the branches of the cucumber plant would bend with the extra weight. Q asked a nearby cucumber, "How can I be sure I won't fall to the ground, if I get too heavy?"

The nearby cucumber smiled and responded, "I wondered the same thing when I was your age. But I learned what would keep me safe."

"What was that?" Q asked.

"A part of our plant is a set of arms that reach out to grab hold of a wire, or a post or a neighbouring plant, to keep our branches secure."

Q thought for a moment and then smiled. "How wonderful it is to have friends and neighbours!" Q exclaimed. And then Q returned to its exercises.

SMALLY THE SEED

THEMES
- Dreams
- Changes to our dreams
- Adapting
- Growing
- Other:

Once upon a time there lived a small seed named Smally.

Smally the seed lived just deep enough under the ground to have lots of worm friends. The worms always wondered why Smally wasn't named "Smiley," since Smally always wore a big smile. So they asked, and Smally said, "It's the dream."

"I can picture myself, a hundred years from now, as one of the widest reaching trees in all the land. My dream is to be able to provide comforting shade for human creatures as they play on bright summer days, or share a picnic, or court each other, or dream of things to be, or maybe just nap in the shade – all under my wide-reaching branches."

The worms were in awe of a dream so big and so far into the future.

And so it was that Smally grew from a small seed to a very wide tree in an open field, with branches reaching out farther than any other tree.

But there was a problem.

The empty field became populated with lots of families, including children, who needed schools, and playgrounds, and houses, and hospitals, and stores, and museums, and more. And as more children climbed on the tree, they sometimes, quite unintentionally, broke some branches. The branches that were left had difficulty growing out because some of the buildings began to get close enough to brush up against them. Some branches were even cut back. Smally wasn't as far reaching as in the old days.

So Smally wondered out loud to the wise eagle who flew above and who always had a wider view of things: "What am l to do about my dream?"

The eagle circled for a while in silence and then answered, "Grow taller."

SUMMER CLOUDS

THEMES
- 🌿 The ending of school
- 🌿 The beginning of summer
- 🌿 Maintaining communication
  with friends while apart
- 🌿 Friendship
- 🌿 Other:

Once upon a time, there were two very good friends named Jamie and Taylor.

They had been best friends for as long as they could remember, but as school ended* it came time to say goodbye. Jamie and Taylor knew they wouldn't see each other all summer long and they were sad about that, but on the way home on the last day of school they made a promise.

They would send a letter to each other every day of the summer.

They walked a few more steps before they realized there was a problem.

They hadn't learned all their letters yet, to say nothing about learning how to write. But they came up with a solution. They would send *pictures* every day, instead.

They walked a few more steps until they realized there was *another* problem.

They didn't have enough money to buy postage stamps for every day of the summer. They walked on a little while further.

It happened to be a beautiful day, and they looked up to see the most wonderful cloud formations.

Jamie said, "Wow, that one looks like a dinosaur!"

Taylor, "I think it looks like an old-style ship, with sails!"

At that moment, they both thought of the same idea. They would use the clouds to send pictures back and forth, every day of the summer.

And so it was that at the same time each day, they would both sit under the same sky, each in their own yard, and look at the clouds and send a picture to their best friend by thought waves.

After about a week of using thoughts to send cloud pictures, a question popped into Jamie's mind: "I wonder if God sends pictures to us this way?"

Jamie decided to ask Taylor about this at the end of the summer.

or as one was moving away, or going to summer camp, or going to spend time with a divorced parent ...

SUNRISE

THEMES
- 🌿 Listening to others
- 🌿 Being tolerant of other views
- 🌿 Compromising
- 🌿 Exploring points of view
- 🌿 Other:

Once upon a time, after a long day of work and play, all the forest creatures came together for a bedtime story.

The story at bedtime was a very special tradition because it was just about the only time all the creatures came together as one community.

There were big, tall, short, and small creatures. There were two-legged, four-legged, and more-legged creatures. They were all very different, yet they shared the same forest, and the story at bedtime reminded them of that fact. It was a time of peace and harmony.

A long-legged spider was the storyteller on this particular occasion. The spider was quite a good storyteller, partly because it could point to several things using its many legs at just the right moment for dramatic effect. There was so much suspense, everyone gave the spider their full attention.

As the story got to the place about a sunrise, one leg dramatically pointed toward the sky as the spider said, "And so the sunrise marked the beginning of a new day."

That's when the argument began.

The creatures who were awake at night argued very loudly that sunrise always marks the *end* of the *night*. The creatures who were awake during the day argued back, equally loudly, that sunrise always marks the *beginning* of a new *day*.

The more they argued, the louder they got.

Finally, someone suggested that this was a good question to ask the wise owl. Asking the owl difficult questions was another long tradition in the forest, because owls can see a lot of things all at once since they live high in trees. Having a wide-eyed view, with very large eyes, helped them see the many sides of an argument.

So it was that the night creatures and the day creatures of the forest presented their cases before the wise owl.

After a moment of silence, which the owl tended to observe in such situations, these words came out, very slowly,

"It ... hap ... pens ... " began the owl ...

All the creatures listened carefully ...

"It ... happens ... that ... all ... of ... you ... are ... right."

For a moment, all the creatures were silent. Then they agreed that they would all have a new and *polite* discussion about why they saw the *same* forest *differently*.

WHICH ONE?

THEMES
* Differences
* Self-identity
* Self-awareness
* Respect for differences
* Other:

Once upon a time ... a very long time ago, a council of angels decided to organize all living beings into three groups: creatures of the air, creatures of the land, or creatures of the sea. The angels set a day for everyone to report which group they belonged to.

On that day, there was a long, long line of different living beings, each waiting for their turn to answer this question, "Which group are you in?"

The first creature in line stepped forward, and the council asked, "Which group are you in?"

"The land group," came the answer.

"Specific type?" came the next question.

"Elephant" the creature replied.

"Next!" one of the angels called out.

The questions and answers continued with each creature in turn.

"Group?"

"Of the air."

"Specific type?"

"Hummingbird"

"Next!"

"Group?"

"Of the sea"

"Specific type?"

"Whale"

All went smoothly, until one creature came forward.

"Group?"

"Of the sea"

But before the angels could ask the next question, the creature kept talking …

"I mean, I *think* I'm of the sea, but I'm also in the land group"

The angels looked confused, but the creature kept talking …

"And I *might* be in the air group as well, but I'm not sure."

The angels were even more confused and responded together, "You can't be all three! You must choose only one."

One of the angel council members suggested a meeting.

After what seemed like forever, the council returned and announced, "We are thankful for this day, as you have taught us a valuable lesson. You don't have to belong to just one group. What shall we call you?"

Someone came up with the name "penguin" for a creature with wings who can walk a long distance and swim in deep waters. And that day the angels celebrated the wonderful differences of creation.

A SIGN OF WISDOM

THEMES
- Benefitting from different points of view
- Listening to others when disagreeing
- Other:

Once upon a time, three forest creatures found themselves in a discussion about the signs of wisdom.

"What is the sign of wisdom?" they asked each other.

The squirrel responded first. "Wisdom is being able to answer 'what' questions really well. For example, '*What* kind of nuts are the best to squirrel away for winter?'"

The deer replied, "It is much more important to be able to answer 'how' questions. For example, '*How* can I avoid hunters when going for a morning stroll?'"

Then the owl spoke: "The sign of wisdom is to be able to answer 'why' questions. For example, '*Why* do we have such different views?'"

The discussion got rather loud, until one of the three suggested that they needed some advice from someone with an outside perspective. So they went to see the eagle, who lived a little outside of the forest. They thought the eagle might have extra wisdom because eagles have good eyes and very clear vision.

They each presented their case to the eagle, who thought about the problem for a while before speaking (itself a sign of wisdom). Finally, the eagle responded: "The true sign of wisdom is knowing the answers to all these kinds of questions – what? how? and why? – *plus* one more thing."

Well, at first the squirrel, the deer, and the owl were silent while they thought about the "*one more thing.*"

What could it be, they wondered to themselves.

The squirrel just had to ask: "What is the 'one more thing'?"

"The one more thing is *sharing*," replied the eagle. "*Sharing* each of the wisdoms you have. For only in *sharing* each piece of wisdom will you be able to gain the *full measure* of wisdom."

The squirrel, the deer, and the owl then returned to the forest a little bit wiser.

EPILOGUE

Storytelling is both a gift and an art. We all possess some portion of that gift, and we all can improve our skill level in the art; we can *all* be storytellers, contributing our questions and insights, and encouraging others of all ages to wonder and reflect upon God's creation.

Although my focus has been on storytelling for religious education, its effectiveness is certainly not limited to that realm. We can use it in all teaching, all parenting, all leadership, and all living (including both personal and social arenas).

May your journey be blessed by being more than a storyteller; may you live so that one day you inspire or become a character in a story told by someone else.

ABOUT THE AUTHOR

Dr. Jed Griswold is an ordained minister in the Christian Church (Disciples of Christ) tradition and has served several pastorates of different denominations. He has also been a college administrator and professor, teaching in the fields of psychology, sociology, philosophy, and religion and has led many workshops on applying the Myers Briggs Type Indicator (MBTI) to educational and religious contexts. He also has a passion for theatre and film – which began with childhood acting and continues today – drawn to the art because stage and film are creative and powerful forms of storytelling. He has written stage scripts and has also appeared in a wide variety of TV pilots, independent films, and feature releases (primarily as an extra), including *Goodwill Hunting*, *Moonrise Kingdom*, and *Spotlight*.

Alphabet of Faith

26 WORDS ABOUT FAITH, ETHICS, AND SPIRITUALITY

SARA JEWELL

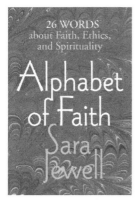

Weaving together faith and culture, this breathtaking book explores what it means to live a life of faith and spirit in the 21st century. It brings together 26 "words" that reflect the challenges and joys of living in our beautiful but broken and often brutal world.

It is unwaveringly contemporary, progressive, and thought-provoking. The pieces are written for those who say they are spiritual but not religious, for people who are or may be familiar with church but perhaps don't attend anymore, for those who know Jesus and his teachings and are familiar with the Bible, even if they haven't opened it in a while.

ISBN 978-1-77343-517-6
256 pages, 4.75" x 7" paperback, $24.95

The Voice of the Galilean

THE STORY OF A LIFE, A JOURNEY, A DISCOVERY, A GIFT, AND A FATE

REX WEYLER

Rex Weyler's *The Voice of the Galilean* stands as one of the most clear, compelling, and concise tellings of the life and teachings of Jesus ever written.

Excerpted and updated from his seminal book *The Jesus Sayings: The Quest for His Authentic Message* – a brilliant synthesis of the work of international Bible scholars and some 200 ancient sources, including the gospels of Thomas and Mary – this book distills the teachings of Jesus with crystal clarity, sensitivity, insight, and passion. Equally important, Weyler challenges readers to bear "witness" to Jesus' message today, in their own lives.

ISBN 978-1-77343-155-0
96 pages, 4.25" x 6.25" paperback, $12.95

WOOD LAKE

IMAGINING, LIVING, AND TELLING THE FAITH STORY.

WOOD LAKE IS THE FAITH STORY COMPANY.

It has told
- the story of the seasons of the earth, the people of God, and the place and purpose of faith in the world;
- the story of the faith journey, from birth to death;
- the story of Jesus and the churches that carry his message.

Wood Lake has been telling stories for 40 years. During that time, it has given form and substance to the words, songs, pictures, and ideas of hundreds of storytellers.

Those stories have taken a multitude of forms – curricula, parables, poems, drawings, prayers, epiphanies, songs, books, paintings, hymns, and more – all driven by a common mission of serving those on the faith journey.

WOOD LAKE PUBLISHING INC.

485 Beaver Lake Road, Kelowna, BC, Canada V4V 1S5

250.766.2778

www.woodlake.com